I Married Him

NOW WHAT?

A Saved Girl's Guide to
Surviving Abusive Marriage

TAKHIA GAITHER

The Ready Write-Her
Baltimore, MD

Disclaimer:

This book is not intended as a substitute for the medical advice of physicians and/or licensed counselors and therapists. The reader should consult a physician in matters relating to his/her mental health and particularly with respect to any symptoms that may require diagnosis or medical attention.

ISBN (Print): 979-8-9881944-4-6
ISBN (Digital): 979-8-9881944-5-3
Library of Congress Number: 2023909259

I Married Him

NOW WHAT?

A Saved Girl's Guide to
Surviving Abusive Marriage

Front cover image by The Ready Write-Her
Book design by The Ready Write-Her

Printed in the United States of America.

First printing edition 2023.

The Ready Write-Her
Takhia Gaither
Subject: Attention – Permissions Requested/Bulk Orders
thereadywrite-her@tsgsgroup.com
thereadywrite-her.com

DEDICATION

This is dedicated to all of the incredibly strong women who became a part of a secret society that we never wanted to join and have their own stories to tell but have been silenced, overlooked, or unheard. I hold space for you.

ACKNOWLEDGMENTS

- To God be ALL the glory. Without Him, I am nothing and I would not be here to write this.

- To my children – my forever "whys." You've seen all the pieces. As much as I don't like that you have, you have also seen me overcome them. Love you to the moon and back again.

- To my family and friends who have prayed for and over me and encouraged me to continue to grow into the woman I am becoming. I love you all and thank you for everything.

- To Antranetta Tillman, Kita Stewart, and Michelle Cameron working with the three of you was where this book started, AnnT – you saw the earliest chapter, Kita – I mapped out the outline, front matter, and the beginning, Michelle – your workshop got me up to chapter 6 so that I all I had to was bring it on home! Your "yesses" helped me get to mine. Thank you!!

- To my coaches, listening ears, and business friends who have continued to hold me accountable, push me, and constantly remind me to stop trippin' and write, there are too many of you to name without forgetting someone, but I pray that you know who you are and that your help has been invaluable.

FOREWORD

When the Lord gives you people in your later years, if you're wise, you recognize and realize that it's for purpose, ON PURPOSE. For me, this was not the case initially. Meeting Takhia was a mere coincidence, but one that was divinely authored and would soon be needed. We both ended up in a group on social media and somehow began chatting outside the group. Little did either of us know, we had married the same type of man and later we joked that they must be brothers.

Each of us journeyed along, sharing stories along the way. While she journeyed in Maryland, and I in Pennsylvania, it never failed that we had so many similar scenarios and the responses to them were almost exactly the same. Being the level-headed, rational women that we are, there were times when we would think away something, there were times when we would process something and then dismiss it, and other times when we would identify a thing for what it was and then compare our strategies for how to best handle it.

Having produced offspring in these types of marriages was both rewarding and simultaneously gut-wrenching as we traversed the highway of "what will it mean for my littles." The joys, tears, unknowns, and fears, weighed equally as we compartmentalized life and what every possible scenario might look like.

Admittedly one looks at the choices ahead and feels all the emotions, and yet looking at those choices is a far cry from making those choices. Each one with its own reality, and despite the well-wishes, and well-meaning thoughts and opinions of others, it has been a comfort to walk the road to wellness, (mental, emotional, and physical), with someone who has "been there, done that" and wrote a book about it!

- *Patricia E. Pritchette*
Author & Editor

TABLE OF CONTENTS

PRELUDE

W ords matter. In today's society, there exists a need to label everything, what you call a thing matters. Thanks to the media we have somewhat taken the meaning away from the word "toxic" and have begun to use it as a synonym when we feel there's a need to be politically correct or polite. It's not ok to call someone or a situation abusive, but you can call it, or them, toxic with very little argument or rebuttal. It's time to call spades, spades. What I, and many others, have endured was beyond toxic, it was abuse and some of us have no physical scars because they're all internal. Toxic was the word we used to hide the abuse that many of us didn't even know we were in until we were out.

Regardless of whatever the relationship was called, I don't fit the profile for it. You know, the one of women that kind of end up in abusive romantic relationships because life at home was dysfunctional and probably abusive, so it's your normal way of life. The one where I made certain decisions regarding men because my father was absent or present but still absent. I wasn't poor, in poverty, or uncared for. None of those things were a part of the story of me. So, how in the world did I end up in a narcissistically abusive marriage??

Well, that my friends, is why we're here today. You see, this is the book that I needed to read some years ago. It is the book that is still very much needed today. Sit back in your comfy chair, grab a pen and a notepad, some tissues (for those of you who are criers), and let's take a little trip. Before we go back to the beginning, let me fast forward to the end and tell you that I am living proof that what the enemy meant for evil, God has worked out for my good (Genesis 50:20).

INTRODUCTION

To be clear, this is not a book about "him," (my ex-husband), or "them," (narcissistic husbands). Yes, there will be examples, there will be definitions, and there will be textbook-level information presented. After all, I am Takhia the Teacher. One of the things that became quite clear as I was traveling along this road is that I wasn't on it for just myself. I began to hear and read stories of countless other women who were, and some still are, in the same type of marriage. For me, everything is a teachable moment. The 5 years of "friendship," 11 years of a situationship, just over 2 years of marriage before it all hit the fan, and the years of walking through a divorce were lesson plans waiting to be written.

So, I repeat, this is not about him or them. It's about me and it's for you. It is to inform, empower, and motivate you to redefine yourself. Why redefine? Because throughout the course of your relationship, I would guess that at this very moment, you are in one of three headspaces:

1. You feel that you are losing yourself.
2. You realize that you have lost yourself.
3. You are starting to regain a sense of normalcy about yourself.

Realistically, there is a strong possibility that you move between these three spaces. I know I did and if I'm honest, it was what infuriated me the most. Especially space 3. Space 3 seems like you should be ready to hit your stride and be done with the whole thing, right? And it was until I realized that it was all a part of the cycle, and I broke it.

Sidebar - Before we get any further, I'm a bit sarcastic and a tad cutthroat at times. Because the nature of this book is for me to help you understand the version of the twilight zone that you're in, I am giving you the real and raw. My real feelings, thoughts, and commentary. I am also granting you permission to do the same with your situation. In reality, you don't need my permission. One of the things that plagued me for a long time was whole-heartedly loving the Lord and even attempting to serve while dealing with the madness of my life and trying to keep it covered up. I had to begin to call it out.

Yes, Jesus knows it all, but to move past it, I had to call it out, give it to Him, and then let Him guide me through it. It required me to be honest, first with Him and then with myself. My prayer for you is that you do the same as you're reading through these pages.

Also, writing was a key part of coming out of this situation. Not to keep a "record of wrong" or to memorialize the events but because writing it out does two things. Number 1, it reactivates your memory. You will need that because if your situation is/was anything like mine, you have spent a lot of time being told that you don't see what you see. Number 2, it gives you a recount of events so that you can begin to put the pieces together of what your cycle looks like. At the end of each chapter, there are notes pages for you to jot down your thoughts.

PART I

The
Beginning

CHAPTER 1
Hindsight

Hindsight is 2020" have never been truer words! Funny now that I think about it but at the time it was anything but laughable. But to paraphrase a line from one of my all-time favorite poems, "…like air I rise."

You've probably been thinking or currently are, "How did I end up in this?" I wonder the same thing about myself all the time. I've come to the loose conclusion that it was a conglomeration of faulty logic, flawed beliefs, and a gift not stewarded properly. I knew all the surface-level things. I knew to not marry an outright non-believer or someone who always treated me poorly outwardly and inwardly. I knew to not be unequally yoked. However, I can and will admit that although I knew the scripture, I messed that whole thing up! I knew that you should love people for who they are and where they were in life, continue to pray for them, and help them where you can.

And this is where my second fault line took off running. In meeting people, if you say to me, "Hey I made these mistakes in life, but I want to learn, grow, and mature to be better," then the teacher in me is going to believe you until you show me otherwise. Meaning you say you want to learn but every time anyone offers you instruction, you don't follow any of it. Or your requests for instruction become requests for me to just do it. And as I told my students often, "I'll help you all day but I'm not going to do it for you." But then comes the small glitch in the matrix where it gets on all my nerves to see someone making an absolute mess, so I take over. In a nutshell, that was the hook. There were too many messes. I should have taken that left at Albuquerque and gone on my way, but instead, I jumped in to try to help save the mess.

The reason I chose to keep trying to fix the mess had nothing to do with "Captain Save-a-Ho" syndrome, (no that is not a psychological diagnosis, but you know those people that always have to jump in and save the day), I didn't have that need. Still don't. I wanted stuff to be over so it could be over, and life could keep moving. The Narcissistic Abuse cycle was a major part of this repeated picture. It consists of three phases: Idealize, Devalue, and Discard. You would think that after discard would be an ending, but in many cases, discard leads to a new beginning.

In the idealization phase, you are the greatest person to ever enter their lives. They just want to be with you all the time, know so much about you, and really get to know you. They sweep you off your feet and everything is rainbows and butterflies. They are so in love and love you so much, life didn't even exist for real before you but now, everything has meaning. The birds are singing, the sun is shining, and it is a brand-new day! Seems really over the top right? They do what's known as love bombing. You're showered with gifts, compliments, care, and so much support that you begin to think you've finally hit the jackpot. This is it! The relationship to end your stint on the dating scene. Things could not be more perfect, almost to the point of being too perfect. And you might find it a little alarming but you're enjoying the ride. Having been taught, "He who finds a wife finds a good thing" and this man is talking about "You are Mrs _____" or "the future Mrs _____," you confidently decide to move forward in the relationship. (If there are some fellas that stumbled across this, first of all, thank you! Second of all, flip everything I say about a "him" to the "her" that you're with or married to. Contrary to belief, there are men who go through these same issues, so this is for you too!)

Then one day in a disagreement about what really doesn't seem to be that catastrophic of an issue, it seems like the whole bottom falls out and you are left confused and bewildered. Need an example? I have them for days! In conversations that couples tend to have we both discussed things that happened in past relationships, good, bad, and indifferent. In an argument that started because he showed up hours late with no real reason as to why, I first got blamed for being perturbed that I'd been waiting for hours and then he pops up like nothing's changed, (the gaslighting of this relationship was horrific but we'll revisit that later). An argument ensues and supposedly ends, I think he might have apologized but I don't really feel like he did. Later in the evening out of nowhere, he says, "Well I see why they all left you. You don't know how to talk to people, you didn't have to come at me like that earlier." Um … what just happened? I thought we'd moved on to the make-up portion of the evening. So now I'm back to trying to pull it together to enjoy the outing when I probably really wanted to punch him in the throat. No, I am not violent nor do I condone it, I just wanted him to shut up and I knew a good throat punch would do it.

That example was kind of minor. There were other times when I was told, "Oh you're not that smart." Or my personal favorite, "Well you don't think well for yourself. So, I need to do that for you." The completely asinine nature of that entire statement has always floored me, and he kept saying it like it was some kind of fact.

Here's the key to the devalue stage. They take things that are known to be your strengths and attempt to disconnect you from them. They also use things that they know have hurt you, to reopen the wound and throw salt in it. You could have just prepared an amazing meal, and everyone is singing your praises and he'll say "Oh that needed some more flavor." Or "My mom's _____ is the best but yours' is ok." Everything you do well there is always someone who does it better. Every issue that you have or have ever had that has been a pain point is because you are horrible or insensitive or insert any negative adjective that you want. Or they've gone through something much worst, so your issue is nothing in comparison. The entire point of it is to make you feel less than. It trains your mind to think that if you are so horrible, then maybe you won't find anyone better than him, and deep inside he really loves you, and you know that one day you can exceed the mark of whoever else is always best.

Before we go into the last stage, stop and take a deep breath. It's a lot. There may be tears, some anger, and a good bit of head nods, combined with that sounds familiar except … Heavy right? It can be but before we continue, I want you to know that you can and will overcome this. You are valuable. You are smart. You are beautiful, inside and out. The opinion of someone who does not have a very high opinion of themselves is of no consequence to you. God says you are worth more than rubies, (Proverbs 31:10). Carry that with you as we move forward through this guide and more importantly, as you move forward through life. So, altogether, breathe in, hold it for 4, and breathe out for 4. (If you need to do this more than once before continuing, do it. Anytime you feel the tension rising, stop, close the book, and just breathe. Come back to it when you're calmer.)

After the usually dumb argument from stage 2 comes the discard stage. I'm not going to lie; this one can be pretty painful. It doesn't matter how many times you see it until you see it. (That'll make sense later!) At this point, you may see the silent treatment, maybe the break-up, the idea that maybe you should take a break, or he'll just ghost out for a few days, talking about "he needed to calm down." This was in the "dating/situationship" phase. In marriage, it was the silent treatment mixed with crazy passive aggression that was still aggression because along with that were these sideways comments, short answers, or digs. In time, to be honest, this became my favorite phase. At one point the silent treatment used to drive me nuts. "Why aren't you talking to me?" "Don't you have something to say?" "I'm really concerned about you, let's talk this out." The day that I got fed up with all of it and realized how much calmer my day was without having to worry about talking, life was good! One of the things that was severely devalued was my independence and the fact that I like to be alone. I like quiet. I don't always want "to people." But because he was always around, I had to concede that, until I just didn't. This whole phase causes you to run and chase after them to earn their love back. And usually, once you've decided to just leave it alone, they come swooping back in and before you know it, you're back at the beginning with the love-bombing and the making-up.

You can end up being on this ride for a while. Sometimes people will convince you that it's just the ups and downs of marriage. I'm going to tell you what my uncle told me as a newlywed going through all of what I just explained to you, "These are NOT newlywed problems. These are not even 5, 10, or 15-year wedded problems. These are NO YEAR problems. They are things that just shouldn't be happening ever at any stage." You are not having marriage problems. You are sitting in the middle of someone else's internal problems that are causing problems in the marriage.

The hindsight is that many of the things I experienced within marriage, I saw them before and had actually planned on walking away from the whole relationship until I thought things would change. There is this thing called the "grand epiphany." It's what happens when some life-altering event takes place and/or they feel that you're really going to leave.

It's beyond love bombing. Love-bombing is overkill. The "grand epiphany" comes across as the most heartfelt apology and statement of life that you've ever heard. It seems so reflective and introspective that you really feel like there will be changes. The changes do take place but they're not permanent. It's the means to an end. The belief is that these are diabolical pre-planned manipulations that have been planned since the first day they met you. Maybe this is still part of my naivety or the fact that I do sincerely want to believe the best of people, in my case, I'm still on the fence about it being pre-planned initially, but I do believe at some point it became the plan. I can't say that I'm sure he was 100% honest, but what I do know now is that my idea of what I was told and his idea of what he was saying were two different things.

For me, if you care and want to move forward you will get your temper in check, you will take responsibility for yourself and your actions; you will be understanding of the demands and needs of the family above your own selfish wants because this is what should happen unconditionally. On the other side, they were all conditional. So as long as I'm not myself, then you won't have a temper problem. As long as taking responsibility for your actions ends with sex, you'll do it. As long as we're doing what you want to do with the money then you're all for it. That was the very fine print on this epiphany.

Of course, once the moment was over and the epiphany faded, we were right back on the wheel. Except this time, it was much worse than before. More high emotions, more vicious speeches, more threats, and just more mess until I called it was and started doing all the research to put this chapter into words so I could tell you about it.

Your Thoughts: Do you know what these phases look like for
you? If so, write it down. If not, just write what you tend to see
and when you tend to see it happen, (i.e on pay day, at times
when you want do something without them, around
holidays/birthdays/significant life days).

_____
_____
_____
_____
_____
_____
_____
_____
_____
_____
_____
_____
_____
_____
_____
_____
_____
_____
_____

_____

_____

_____

_____

_____

_____

_____

_____

_____

_____

_____

_____

_____

_____

_____

_____

_____

_____

_____

_____

_____

_____

_____

_____

_____

_____

_____

_____

_____

_____

CHAPTER 2
Why You??

Loaded question. Why did they come to you with this madness? Why are you allowing it? Why, why, why?? (Insert Whitley podium breakdown from the debate episode of "A Different World.") Honestly, it may take a while to actually realize the answer, and to be even more honest, if you're waiting for him to answer any of it, you'd sooner grow gills and become a fish. In the beginning, his responses to any why question will seem almost logical or make some variation of sense, but that's usually after you're so mentally worn out that the alphabet sung out of order might actually make sense.

Back to the original premise, we can't answer for him. He might not even know for real. We can only deal with our own "whys." This can be where the "fun" starts. I have always been very introspective, so when things start looking out of sorts, I evaluate EVERYTHING, me included. Having also been pretty self-critical, I made it a point to evaluate myself far better than anybody else. I gave other people the benefit of the doubt, myself not so much. Given my natural demeanor combined with the inaccurate stories about me being repeated back to me, I became extra critical. Maybe you find yourself in this same space or you've been there before. It's ok if that's the case, it's hard but we can work through it. Keep in mind that it is important to extend the grace to yourself that you so easily give to others.

Each of us will have our own set of "whys" but here are some common threads that I have either witnessed, read about, or heard in conversation after conversation. All of them do not apply to everyone. Why did they pick us? What is it that attracted them to us and us to them? These are not in any particular order but are numbered for clarity:

1. You seemingly had everything going for yourself - You were Webbie's "Miss I. N. D. E. P. E. N. D. E. N. T." You had your stuff together - stable job/career, lived alone, in school or degreed. That was probably your ringtone or if you like something smoother, Neyo's Miss Independent or the remix with

Jamie Foxx. You were that girl. You didn't "need" a man in that sense, but you wanted and needed a companion, a friend, a love.

2. You are highly empathetic - Being empathetic is not spooky or mystical. As a Christian, we should not claim the label of "empath." Long story short, the origins of the term are not godly at all. Back to the point, you have the ability to feel people's feelings. You are "rejoice with those who rejoice" and "cry with those who cry," (Romans 12:15) in the flesh. It's just a natural part of who you are. And for those who cry, you immediately want to jump in and help resolve, solve, or rectify the situation. What you have is a gift untrained, we'll talk more about that later.

3. You had or have daddy issues - I am not saying this to be derogatory or hurtful, it's the truth. If your father did not perform his role of leading, protecting, providing, and covering at any time in your life, when you meet a man who says he will do or shows he might do these things, you latch on because you don't know

what it actually looks like for this to happen in ways that are healthy and productive.

4. You held marriage as an idol - This comes in a few forms. Girls dream of their wedding days from like forever. You watch Cinderella or any other fairytale and think that your prince will come and don't even realize that happily ever after is never discussed or that it might involve problems, just because life has problems. Chick flicks and 90's R&B have you thinking that you're just supposed to be in love through trash and it's ok because that's what makes love and life real. Or you just wanted so badly to be married, maybe the clock was ticking, or maybe like me you already had kids, so the next logical step was to get married.

I was 1, 2, and 4. Thank God 3 was not a factor because, for me, that was a big part of what started my transition out, (thanks Dad! I appreciate you more than you know).

Because I was Miss Independent, one of the things that came up often was "Oh you don't need a man." Younger more arrogant me said, "You're right I don't." Older, slightly less arrogant me said, "You're wrong. I don't need one for what

you think or what you're giving. But I do need the right one."
Either response sparked an argument but the last one always
struck a nerve. There are 2 things that most narcissistic men
usually pride themselves on, #1 - is having what appears to be
a large amount of expendable income, and #2 - is their
performance in the bedroom. So, what do you do with a
woman like me who makes her own coins and could care less
about sex?? You try to make her feel less than for both. And
that's exactly where I was and married because I loved him,
and we have children, and I believed the grand epiphany from
Chapter 1. (I really feel like the epiphany needs its own
chapter. It wasn't on my original list, but some time should
definitely be spent there.)

Breathing time. Take a minute to decompress. This is
also a good time to journal out your why. It may cause you to
be angry, there may be tears and even sadness. Pray it through
and allow yourself to feel. Ignoring the why is your new
reaction to ignoring you. You must pay attention to yourself.
If this piece is too difficult for you to face, deal with, or walk
through on your own, call a counselor, therapist, or coach. It is
ok to not be ok and it is ok to need help to get there. I'll include
some options in the resources section.

You ready to keep going?? One more big one and then
we'll get to some solutions. The last big why … Why do you
stay? Again, not a cookie-cutter answer or rationale. Here's a

giveaway - the title of this book. Far too often in churches has been the war cry to stay in abusive marriages. Far too often the belief has been shared, passed down, and drilled in that as a wife you must stay regardless of what he does. Far too often is the misnomer emphatically told that you being a helpmate means that you are supposed to help him realize his cruel and intolerable behavior. And while all of this is going on, your only recourse is to pray and wait on God.

But that's just one piece. Maybe your church, family, or circle of friends has no idea what you are currently living through. You hide it well or at least well enough that even if no one particularly believes that everything is fine, they leave it alone because you're the person that rarely involves anyone in the personal intimate details of their lives anyway. So basically, you're suffering in silence. Conversely to this is that you have said something, but you were met with everything under the sun about why the Bible says you can't go and/or my personal favorite, "You knew that before you got married," which all equates to just suck it up until death do you part. But what no one realizes is that you're slowly dying. You are losing every shred of anything that ever resembled you. Your drive, your ambition, your go-get-it-ness, (yes I made up a word), your resilience.

I can admit that my own faulty logic about marriage had a big impact on why I stayed. I was met with all the scriptures. The pep talks about how to do whatever it is that he is asking, and things will be just fine after it works itself out. I had to have some heart to hearts with God and myself. I used to always say for certain situations, me and Jesus would have to sit and have coffee about that. Considering at the time, I didn't drink coffee, I never made time for the conversation. During the course of my marriage, I started having coffee with Jesus every morning. I needed to know HIS heart for me, for my marriage, for my life period. This book, Be the Overcomer, and chapters in over 10 anthologies were the result of my coffee sessions. I had questions, He answered and He's still answering. I came to Jesus when I was 12 and got the Holy Ghost at 14, but in the middle of a disaster of a marriage, I had my real come to Jesus moment. Look up the scriptures for yourself, all of the ones that discuss marriage and the biblical outs. But also, read the book of Proverbs, (I have a link for a really good study guide, I'll include it as a resource and some other scriptures as well). To get this "why," you have to know what you know, what you believe, and what you were taught, and then understand that those three things can be very different. My reminder to you is that this work is not going to be easy. But you can do it. It's your pace that you set with the Father. Remember, there is always help available.

Your Thoughts: Take some time to think about your whys and if they arise, the hows as well.

_____

_____

_____

_____

_____

_____

_____

_____

_____

_____

_____

_____

_____

_____

_____

_____

_____

_____

_____

_____

_____

_____

_____

_____

_____

_____

_____

_____

_____

_____

_____

_____

_____

_____

_____

_____

_____

_____

_____

_____

_____

_____

_____

_____

_____

CHAPTER 3
The Grand Epiphany

You know in movies when someone is in a near-death situation and suddenly their whole life flashes before their eyes and after they escape death, they come out of the situation a brand-new person? Think Jim Carey at the end of "Liar, Liar," if you need a frame of reference. That's what it feels like to be in the grand epiphany moment. But unlike movies, things don't work out the way you think they should or will.

By the time you get to a grand epiphany moment, your husband has probably smoothed you over one too many times about an incident that keeps reoccurring. Each time you're fed up to the point of leaving but somewhere in the heat of the argument or time frame to become one step closer to release, your "fatal flaw" takes over and you don't leave or if he leaves, you let him back in. Now I hear you and I see the neck rolls, "What do you mean fatal flaw?" 'You said this was not a book to shame the victim. I ain't done nothing wrong!!" (Yes, I'm a whole teacher, writer, and editor and just used the word ain't ... sure did!) Just go with me. Quotes are important. Your "fatal flaw" is not actually fatal. In most cases, you have done nothing wrong. You've had a natural response and reaction to some level of outrageousness but in the aftermath and the calm, it's presented back to you as an overreaction or a trigger for them.

I'll give you an example. The Valentine's Day before we separated I needed a "me" day. I called out of work and spent the day at a corner table in Panera Bread doing homework, catching up on some webinars that I wanted to listen to, grading papers, and putting together lesson plans and outlines. It was a very productive time and things were going great until I got a call from my husband. Since I was "at work" I swiped the call and sent back a message for him to text me because I couldn't talk. For whatever reason, he'd called my job and the secretary told him that I was out for the day, and in the words of one of my favorite episodes from the TV show A Different World, "And that's when the fight broke out!" Almost literally. He came to the Panera and caused a whole scene. It was craziness, complete and utter craziness. In his "I'm sorry" speech, the whole incident was and still is my fault

I Married Him NOW WHAT?

because I lied to go on a date at Panera. (When he got there, I was seated at a table that was full of books, papers, notebooks, and 2 laptops and I was facing the wall! Nothing about the setting said date.) In his world, we separated because I wanted to be able to see whoever I went on the date with. He was slightly right, I did want to be able to see myself without dealing with his foolishness because I took the day to date me.

My fatal flaw, I lied. I wasn't at work, I was at Panera, still working but at Panera. But the question I asked myself afterward was "Why was it even a necessity to have to lie to get a day of peace?" Because had I told the truth my day would have been worse, so even looking back at it, just having those 5 hours of peace and productivity was worth more to me than anything else. I've said all of that to point out that your "fatal flaw" might be something that's wrong but in the moment of you doing it, it was a necessity or the best wrong thing you could do. Should I have lied? No. Should you scream in arguments? No. Should you say things that are rude and callous? No. But do all of them happen, especially when you're in survival mode? Yes, they do, and more often than you care for them to happen.

When you're in this frame of mind, is usually when the epiphany comes. You are done, over it, ready to end it, maybe have said it's over and not just completely gone through with separating or filing papers. It comes in like a breath of fresh air. It's everything that you want to hear but at the same time, you feel a nudge not to believe it. But you really want to believe it. You know there is a change coming. This time is going to be it. You will not be back down this road again. Life from now on will be different. Your prayers have been answered.

For a few months, maybe even years if you're "lucky" the epiphany is real. The behavior changes. The relationship appears to be more reciprocal than one-sided. You are feeling valued and appreciated as a wife. It is an awesome feeling. Then you start to notice little things that begin to unravel like strings on t-shirts. The little nit-picky things that had gone away, now start to come back up. You may notice inconsistencies in stories, the snippy comments, the silent treatment, and the passive aggression, all start to return. You address them and the gaslighting starts all over again. "No I'm not staying out later, that's just because work is demanding right now." "No I'm not talking to her anymore, what are you talking about?" "No I'm not drinking, my homeboy left that in the car. I just had a sip with him to celebrate." Before you know it, life in the epiphany is over and you are once again back to this place of asking why you? How'd you get here? What brought this on?

Let's take a breath. I know it's heavy. Give yourself some space here. Start with the pages at the end of the chapter or get your journal and write it out. Just have a brain dump. To begin to overcome these things you have to recognize what they are and what they look like. This is not an exercise to dwell on past events, it's for you to reflect. Summarize the events, your feelings, your "fatal flaws," and anything else that you can think of surrounding the situations. I bring up the grand epiphany early on in the book because you have to stop the cycle but in order to stop it you have to recognize the pieces and when you could potentially be on the road back into it. Before moving on to part 2, sit here for a while. If you need to talk this out, check out the resources section.

Your Thoughts: *Brain dump time! Just let it all out.*

_____

_____

_____

_____

_____

_____

_____

_____

_____

_____

_____

_____

_____

_____

_____

_____

_____

_____

_____

_____

_____

_____

_____

_____

_____

_____

_____

_____

_____

_____

_____

_____

_____

_____

_____

_____

_____

_____

_____

_____

_____

_____

_____

_____

_____

PART II

Sorting Through It

CHAPTER 4
What Am I Dealing With?

We spent the beginning of this book talking about the things you've probably seen, dealing with some emotions, and building some ah-ha moments. Now it's time to understand what you could be dealing with. Narcissism is a media buzzword. Every time you turn around the label is given to someone for some reason. Sometimes it fits, most times though, it really doesn't. Society mostly focuses on the inflated ego, the need for constant attention, and some of the power dynamics, real or imaginary, (as exhibited by a recent prominent politician). However, megalomaniacs have some of these same traits. It's more than the extreme love of self and vanity, it's an entire clinical diagnosis that is actually hard to diagnose because most people who display the traits usually don't/won't ever go to therapy.

Narcissism is titled after the character Narcissus in Greek mythology. Narcissus was gorgeous, handsome if you will, but he was obsessed with his own looks. At the same time a nymph, Echo, (in some versions this person is a young man), was hopelessly in love with Narcissus. He ignored her so much for his own image, that eventually she faded away and all that was left of her was her voice. This is a loose variation of this story because as you know with Greek mythology there are many versions, small details, and entanglements. As Echo faded away, Narcissus met his demise when he walked by a pond and caught a glimpse of his own reflection. Attempting to get closer and closer to it, he fell in and drowned.

Narcissistic Personality Disorder, NPD, the technical name for what we commonly call narcissism, is a DSM-5 classified personality disorder. The DSM-5 is the abbreviation for the Diagnostic & Statistical Manual of Mental Disorders written by the American Psychiatric Association, APA. According to the APA, NPD is defined as a pattern of need for admiration and a lack of empathy for others in which a person may have a grandiose sense of self-importance, a sense of entitlement, and they may take advantage of others or have an obvious lack of empathy. A diagnosis of NPD can only be obtained from a licensed counselor/therapist/doctor when the person displays at least five, (5), of the following 9 characteristics:

1. A grandiose sense of self-importance.

2. A preoccupation with fantasies of unlimited success, power, brilliance, beauty, or ideal love.

3. A belief that he or she is extremely special and unique and should only associate with or be surrounded by others who are equally special or go to places with high levels of esteem, specialness, or uniqueness.

4. A need for excessive admiration.

5. A sense of entitlement.

6. Take advantage of others to achieve their personal needs.

7. A lack of empathy.

8. A belief that others are envious of him or her.

9. Extremely arrogant or haughty behaviors or attitudes.

I am providing this information for you to be able to put some things into context. Part of your healing will be understanding who/what you are dealing with. Additionally, I do not want you to start, or increase, the number of side-eyes thrown toward your husband. Understanding that these things are present will help you if/when you seek additional help and counseling, (which I highly recommend), to have language for things you may be experiencing.

It is also important for you to know that while your marriage may definitely be toxic, you may not be married to a person with NPD. There are those who do not meet the requirements for the DSM-5 classification but display narcissistic traits. The second thing I want you to know is that realistically, you may not ever know if he has NPD. This is where knowledge is power. When I began to see my clinician, being the researcher and teacher that I am, I literally walked into the office with printouts of articles, my psychology textbook, and notes of examples because I had questions. Since he was not present, nor was he being seen by a clinician, they could not and would not diagnose him, they could only develop my treatment plan based on the information I presented. This is also the information they will not give you voluntarily as no one wants to be sued for malpractice or slander in "diagnosing" someone they've never worked with. Given the information you present and based upon your mental state and what you are experiencing when you come to them, if asked, they should be able to confirm or deny if at the very least you've been in contact with someone who could potentially be diagnosed or not.

As we move forward, we'll talk more about what these 9 things may look like on a day-to-day basis. You may not see them all the time, but let's be clear, being in a relationship where you feel a lack of empathy, feel that you're being used, always being made to feel less than, or you experience any of the other things above is not ok. Even if your relationship cannot be classified as a by-product of narcissism, it is toxic and that is not healthy for anyone involved, and it is especially dangerous to you and your children if you have any. This is not to scare you or question your motherhood. Remember, I am not here to judge you, I have been a version of you. We'll talk more about forgiveness later, but throughout this process, you must be willing to forgive yourself. Give yourself the grace and benefit of the doubt that you've shown countless times to many others. If it helps, let James Fortune's "I Forgive Me," minister to you.

One last thing and this one is an important matter of safety. Even if your husband has not been physically violent towards you, approaching him with this information may ignite a sense of rage and a plethora of other highly volatile actions. There is a lot to unpack here. My job is to provide you with as much info as I can so that if there comes a time when you must confront this large elephant in the room, you are prepared mentally, emotionally, and perhaps physically, if necessary, (not for violence, more so for location). Do the best that you can to not engage him in any debate, argument, or combative battle about narcissism and its symptoms. It will be counterproductive. One reason is because they believe there's nothing wrong with them and they're perfect. Reason two is because they function at such high levels of manipulation, they will take the information and lead you to believe that you are in fact narcissistic just because you asked them.

CHAPTER 5
Empty Shells

A s I started this chapter, I had one train of thought in mind. However, having had a moment to sit with this concept of empty shells, I now see a bit of duality. There are two meanings - one for us and one for them. (No this is not war and we are not opponents.) I am not one to shame anyone, so this is no judgment on either side. I will repeat often, it's my broken record line, when you know what you're dealing with, you can act accordingly. Be sure to journal through this information. Let's get to work!

Have you ever cracked an egg that had nothing in it? I don't eat eggs but somewhere growing up I actually saw it happen and it was the weirdest thing ever. You would think that the shell would have disintegrated or just fallen apart. Sometime later, I think I asked some farmer at a fair and he said that sometimes in the early stages of egg laying, there is a small hole in the shell that allows the contents to leak out. There may not be a visible crack and the hole can be really small. The reason why there is no evidence of the leak is that the chicken will actually lick up the contents of the spilled egg and keep sitting on it like nothing ever happened. This is how it feels to deal with them. We're the egg, sitting empty. They are the chicken sitting proudly on what they know has been eaten alive and will not hatch.

I'll speak for myself. This was a huge point of contention for me. Prior to getting married, I was pretty established. I'd started a career, bought a house, had 2 degrees, and was working on a 3rd and although life wasn't perfect I was doing ok. Being an introvert, I've always been the chic that will go to a party and sit in the corner watching, (partly because I shouldn't have been there to start with but anyhow ...), because I just wanted to get out for a bit, and then go back home. During the time of my situationship and then marriage, I watched "the life" get sucked out of me. Everything was an issue. Even going to church was problematic. Like who has a problem with Jesus? Really?

The more I fought to hold on to pieces of me the more they seemed to disappear. If I'm honest, I was worn out before the marriage, which is how I missed all the flags that said don't go. I thought the epiphany was it and things would be different and better. What revealed the emptiness was being married for less than 6 months and repeatedly hearing my husband scream at me, sometimes in front of other people, (the children included), "I should have never married you." Each time it was like a knife reopening a wound, the day it slit me clear open and there was nothing left was the day he screamed it in front of my mother. It should have been the end, but I was soo … just so. I can't even find the words to describe anything about anything at that moment. I was empty. Vacant. Hollow. A walking, talking, breathing, empty shell. Days later, he wanted to hover, be my friend, and have date night to make up, while I was still completely empty.

The emptiness is a huge distraction. Realistically distraction probably isn't even the right word to describe it. I was legitimately foggy. I couldn't cry and wasn't sure if I really wanted to. My memory was done, my thoughts were done, and my focus was non-existent. My focus being nonexistent was a huge flag for me because, over time, I'd learned to build focus in adversity. In "Be the Overcomer" I discussed how I battled depression with no therapist. Part of how I managed to do it was that I would throw myself into work. It became a defense and avoidance mechanism. When life was horrible, I would get another job or take another class. I'd do anything but be idle enough to have to deal with it. That only worked for so long, at some point, I had to stop running and face the emptiness. There were not enough classes to fill that void.

The Sunday following his screaming match was women's day at what became our church. We walked in and sat in the back. I don't recall ever singing so loud and listening so intently in service ever, but I was all in that day. I have never been one to make trips to the altar because I didn't want people in my business. God said go, I picked up all the pieces of my broken, empty self and walked up to the altar. I can't remember all of what was said to me but in key moments, I see and hear the words very clearly when I need them. What I remember is being bent over almost doubled and in pain but by the end, I walked upright and came up with a new determination.

Being an empty shell is more harmful than you know. These relationships, (not the actual people), are sent to destroy purpose. The empty shell leaves you vacant and wondering why you're even here. It is the beginning of what could be a very steep decline … BUT GOD!

At this moment, if you are feeling that you are an empty shell, I encourage you to make an altar where you are, if you don't want to or can't speak your prayers, write them out. Even if you can speak, writing is therapeutic, you should write it down. Pour out your heart to God. Make the decision to give Him all your broken pieces. He knows the plans for you, they are for good and not for harm, (Jeremiah 29:11).

48

Your Thoughts: The prayer for mending broken pieces.

_____

_____

_____

_____

_____

_____

_____

_____

_____

_____

_____

_____

_____

_____

_____

_____

_____

_____

_____

_____

_____

_____

_____

CHAPTER 6
Empty Shells, Part 2

Now that you have an idea of what's happening or has happened to you, let me take a minute to present what's happening on the other side. Here is where I go into teacher mode. I can't present just one side of a situation. My job is to make sure that you are aware of all the needed and necessary information to make informed decisions and choices. Whether your husband is saved or identifies as a Christian or not, there are some key things that will hopefully begin to make sense as you continue reading.

As I mentioned at the start of the last chapter, "empty shells" actually has two meanings. It is how we are left to feel but is also how they feel all the time. In an attempt to fill their own voids, narcissistic people seek to cut down everyone they may feel inferior to. A few chapters back I mentioned that I was a pretty stable person prior to this relationship. That was something that he was not. They tend to take your strengths and position them as weaknesses because they are weak at those things themselves. For me, excelling in school was and still is a strength, for him it was not. While he's always known of my accomplishments and degrees, at other times in life I've never really talked much about them because it was a deterrent when meeting new people. At the beginning of our friendship/relationship, he would constantly tell me how impressed he was with my educational efforts and use them as bragging points. Any girl would feel flattered that her man was giving her props out in public but that wasn't really what it was. My accomplishments were great because they made him look good. During the course of our marriage, I started and finished a degree program and his true feelings about my education came to the forefront. I graduated Summa Cum Laude I think, and to this day he's never said anything about it other than to make snide or sideways remarks about being in school. When I think back, it had been that way for a long time about any accomplishment, including birthdays and sometimes holidays. If it highlighted me, it was seldom celebrated by him.

In many instances, there are definite cases of what is known as "arrested development." No, not the cool singing group from the '90s or the tv show which appeared on Fox and

Netflix. It's a psychological event that takes place during a particular age of psychological development. For example, if someone experiences a traumatic event at the age of 8, while they may appear to have recovered from it, and healed outwardly, you will see traces of an 8-year-old's thought patterns their entire life. In a person exhibiting traits of narcissism, this is highly prevalent. A lot of their thought processes don't develop past the age of the traumatic event so the ability to use logic and reason effectively is altered which will reflect in their actions, tantrums, blow-ups, and extreme emotional instability.

It's also a point where the behaviors that we see when we're adults begin to develop. In the case of men, the incidences vary. There are stories of near-death experiences, horrible accidents, the death or incarceration of a parent, and the traits of a narcissistic parent "taught" to the child. Sidebar - mothers of sons ... I know they are our babies, but we have to keep in mind that who we are raising will one day be somebody's husband. We can't teach him to be a man, but we can teach him to be a respectable, responsible God-fearing adult who treats his wife and anyone else with the utmost respect. Spoiling them ridiculously because they're young kings doesn't quite accomplish that. Teach them accountability, which is probably a trait you have not witnessed often in their father. Not telling you how to raise your children, just giving some perspective to things you may see regarding their behaviors. But back to the grown-ups ...

They carry this emptiness with them throughout life, but it's perpetuated by others telling them they are better and above anyone else and deserve the best of everything excessively or they create an internal thought pattern that says they should. The result is living in a series of lies all created in their own minds. They are the best and everything they touch or come in contact with will be or should be perfect. Everything must meet their expectations and standards which are forever changing. The lack of empathy means they will stomp all over anyone in the way of them achieving this perfection. You either live up to what they want or face the wrath of the adult tantrum that comes from not doing so.

It's really eye-opening to see them through the context of "life" that happened to them as opposed to all they are "doing" to you. It takes work and a lot of prayer. In fact, prayer is what keeps bitterness and hatred from forming in you. I asked God to show me what I'm missing about him that has all of this coming at me. When He showed me, He made it clear to give me the caution, warning, and directive that I CANNOT heal or save him, that is HIS job and His job alone. I share that same message with you today. It is not our job to heal broken men. In believing that we are "helping" God, we are breaking ourselves and allowing ourselves to be broken by someone who has no interest in repairing us or being a part of our healing process.

I repeat this is not information you take or present to him. Now you may point out individual events or things that you say, but because the word narcissist in any form is such a buzz word you will be met with unparalleled opposition. While narcissism is a psychological occurrence, it has very demonic ties. This is not a demon that you throw some oil on, say a prayer, speak in tongues for a little bit, and it's cast out. Understand that depending on your house of worship, that may be the answer that you get. There's nothing wrong with it but in this situation, it's ineffective. He has to be willing to renew his mind and close the door to it.

The entire situation calls for Jesus and therapy. We believe and have faith all day, but we also have to come out of this mindset that Jesus is sitting somewhere waiting to go "Shazam!" to fix all our problems. Some things He does on His own, others He works through people. Many who are going through these things internally, rarely see counselors of any kind, therapeutic or pastoral. They don't believe they need them, everyone else is the problem. They are victims of everyone else's issues. Remember, there's a lack of empathy, as such they will not see, and have no interest in seeing, the trail of damage they've left behind them. In their minds, it's all justified.

This is for your awareness to pray on how to proceed. It is to give you language for what you may be seeing and experiencing. Remember G.I. Joe, "Knowing is half the battle." That really is true with this. Knowing allows you to begin the process back to reality and come out of the fog. As we close out this section, take some time to journal. You may also want to check out the resources for additional information. Be aware of information overload, there is a rabbit hole that is so easy to fall down. As with all things, pray for guidance and allow the Lord to direct your research. When He gives the stop, STOP!

Your Thoughts: The prayer for mending broken pieces.

_____

_____

_____

_____

_____

_____

_____

_____

_____

_____

_____

_____

_____

_____

_____

_____

_____

_____

_____

_____

_____

_____

_____

_____

PART III

Coming Out of the Dark

CHAPTER 7
The Exhaustive Toll

In the world of teaching, we do this thing called backward planning. In planning a unit, after you've decided what you will be teaching, you create the exam first and then create the lessons that will cover those topics. I'm going to take a variation of that approach with this chapter. Ready, here we go!

Summer 2022 - Present	Walking in Victory! No more bondage!! ( )
Summer 2022	Divorced
Late 2021	Filed for divorce
Late 2020	Separated
Spring 2018	Married

Summer 2007 - Spring 2018 Situationship

Spring 2002 - Summer 2007 Just Friends

Take a quick glance back at the title of this chapter and now check out this timeline "one mo' 'gain." There's some movie where the lady narrator starts off by saying, "I was a young girl when we met…" I feel like it's maybe the TV version of "Their Eyes Were Watching God," but I digress. Even in typing it all out, the first thing I said was "Geesh that's long!" Right now, if you're considering your personal timeline and begin to feel heavy, close the book and walk away for a bit. Allow yourself time to process. I'm not giving you advice that I haven't had to take in writing. Take some moments and breathe. Revisit those affirmations from earlier to remind yourself who God says you are. In case you hear that little voice whispering, "You won't get out." Tell it to beat it! You are an overcomer in the name of Jesus!

Some may feel the timeline isn't important. But it really is and here's why:

1. It's a reminder/realization that everything you're feeling did not happen overnight. It took time to get from the "magical beginning" to the end.
2. Perspective is important. One of the things that made it hard to break the abuse cycle was the fact that I kept

going back to the place where we were friends. That place is a mind trap, I'll talk more about it in a bit.

3. I wanted to address the pink elephant up front - yes there was a divorce. Without it, I would not be here. You need to know God loves you more than a broken covenant.

Twenty years is a long time to know a person. It feels even longer when you begin to think back and wonder if or even realize that the entire time you were being groomed to be in the very space that you're in. The space where you're worn out, undone, a shell of yourself, and desperately wanting a way out but not sure how to find it or if you're able to take it. I get it, and I pray every answer you need and every way you need to be made, God reveals and sends them to you.

I'm going to ask you a question and I want you to sit with this a little bit. Don't become frustrated if you can't answer but acknowledge the fact that you can't. Are you exhausted? Sleep only partially cures what ails you, you are just in this state of perpetual tiredness. Red Bull does not give you wings for very long, 5-hour energy taps out after 2, Rock Star seems like a jazz band, and Monster is the equivalent of Casper the friendly ghost. I can honestly say I experienced all of that. I didn't even realize a lot of it was happening until the separation. At one point, I'd literally built up any immunity of sorts to Red Bull. I could drink one, take a 2-hour nap and then get up energetic, but the fact that I could drink it and go to sleep was a clear indicator that I'd had too much.

There have been studies conducted that show that living in prolonged states of trauma is not only mentally depleting, but it's physically depleting as well. Think about it, in a day you may go from feeling happy, to anxious because they called with some annoyance, to relieved because the annoyance was solved, to stressed out because now it's time to go home and you know the resolved annoyance is going to come back up in an unpleasant conversation. You spend the rest of the night trying to calm down, recenter, and return yourself to a state of peace so that you won't have troubled rest, although sometimes, you can't reach that level of calm, so you just go to sleep in whatever state you're in. Then you get up the next day and start it all over. It's like a real-life version of "Ground Hog's Day" with Bill Murray except it is anything but comical and we don't see an end. Does any of this sound familiar?

Living this pattern repeatedly walks you right into survival mode. I was going to include details about it in this book, but it really needs its own space. Survival mode is where your brain decides to live so that you are not overtaken by the craziness that is or has become your life. Every human has a survival instinct. Your will to live is supposed to kick in.

What's not supposed to happen is that you treat every day like an emergency experience where you have to do whatever you can to just survive. It's like "12 Years a Slave" meets Survivor, isn't their tagline only the strong win or something like that? Day in and day out, you find yourself making these emergency decisions even when there's no emergency present. The reality is that you're trying to avoid the emergency so you do all you can to pre-plan for it not to happen. Sadly, more times than not, your efforts are shot with flaming darts laced with gasoline.

Until you are either outside of the situation or someone else points it out, you usually don't know that this is where you are. Prior to getting married, I kind of knew I was in this mode, but I didn't know what to call it. I just knew I didn't like it and I didn't want to be there. In my naivety, I thought getting married would shake it and break it. And for a few months, it did. Things were going well until 2 or 3 months in when I noticed some old behaviors creeping back in. By 6 months, if I had been coherent enough to realize it, I would've tried to file for an annulment, but I was so frazzled that I miscounted the number of months I'd been married.

The exhaustion is what drew me back to the Father. It was the space where I began to regain control of myself. I started reading and studying more. I definitely prayed more. And I started writing more. I needed God to be everything because I was down to nothing. All of my meters were off. I was regaining control of my emotions but for most of the first year, I was an emotional wreck, for year 2, I refused. My health was impaired from all the stress, anxiety, and high incidences of anger, which then triggered another medical condition. Mentally, I wanted to be focused and ok, but I absolutely was not. However, I was a functional depressant. No one ever knew what I had going on.

If you're in this space now, then make today the day that you decide to come home to the Father. He's waiting for you. Hand Him all your stuff, He can take it. You don't have to feel like you need to dive right in and petition for sainthood. You can start small. I started by reading the YouVersion verse of the day and I would journal about what the verse said to me. I also started listening to the Bible every time I got in the car. I was doing one of the Bible in a Year plans. When I was in the car alone, it'd be my time with God. Small beginnings produce big results.

Take the space here to really answer this question as honestly as you can. You ready??

HOW ARE YOU??

And as I like to say to my friends, real answers only. Not the ones we're trained or programmed to say because we don't want anyone else involved in our crazy. Or the answers we've learned from speaking "church-an-ese" so the answer to everything becomes "Blessed and highly favored," which it's fine to be, but you can be tired, blessed, and highly favored. They're not mutually exclusive events. You can be all those things at the same time.

Your Thoughts: *How are you?*

_____

_____

_____

_____

_____

_____

_____

_____

_____

_____

_____

_____

_____

_____

_____

_____

_____

_____

_____

_____

_____

CHAPTER 8
The Expected End

For I know the plans I have for you, "declares the Lord, "plans to prosper you and not to harm you, plans to give you hope and a future," Jeremiah 29:11, the NIV version. The end of the King James version says, "… thoughts of peace, and not evil, to give you an expected end." This became the scripture that I measured my life against. I could not figure out what was God and what wasn't. My radar was completely off. You may find yourself in that same space.

I cannot tell you whether to divorce or not because that's a conversation best had between you and the Lord. In my case, after much prayer and going back and forth with myself, I heard Him whisper, "It's ok to let go."

Because we got married to be married and do life as a wife, no matter how bad it is or seems, there will be something in us that wants to keep trying. It's who we were made to be. In general, women were designed to be helpers. We've been told for a good portion of our lives that our purpose in life was to be married and raise God-fearing children. Divorce in marriage is not an option. No matter how bad it is, you keep praying, plant yourself, and stay.

Every time I hear that advice though, I cringe and roll my eyes loudly. Not because it's not true but it really is more damaging than we realize. Prayer is always important, needed, and necessary. In situations where the abuse is physical, very few people question why you're leaving or why you need to leave. However, when you are enduring and/or have endured the beatings that leave scars unseen to the eye, your judgment suddenly becomes questionable to those on the outside. Especially when the smear campaign begins to tell the world that "You were a horrible wife and never wanted to be married to begin with." Or the narrative that you're an opportunist and only got married for whatever material gain there may have been or insert any other set of lies. I'm sure you have a list of things you can insert that you've heard about yourself. Following that advice begins to make you feel like God's not listening to you. Well, I'll be honest, that was my feeling. A cross between that and I'm just not going to bother God about this mess again.

Here's the thing. When you begin to apply the scriptures to your life, you begin to realize that God said what He said and meant what He meant. If His plans are never for our harm, then why would He leave us in the "care," (and I use that term loosely), of someone who consistently piles on the damage?

In the resources section, I'm going to provide you with a list of scriptures to read, pray into, and study on your own to assist with your decision. The people perish for a lack of knowledge, (Hosea 4:6 paraphrased), because of poor teachings and not seeking to learn for themselves. Growing up in church, we could only learn what was available. In adulthood, I began to realize that what was available was subjective to someone else's views and experiences. We need to develop or redevelop our own history with God. We can no longer afford to go on the Sunday School lessons of our youth. We have to begin to dive in for ourselves. I know that may seem hard when some days you really wonder whether or not you know your name or what day of the week it is.

Additionally, I cannot tell you how or when you'll reach your endpoint. I wish there was a mathematical formula or a computer program that I could crank out to give you an exact answer. (Man, if I could make one of those …but I digress). You cannot calculate nor can you take an accurate measurement of human feelings to quantify a program output.

Here is what I can say. You'll know when you know. That sounds very cryptic, to the point of being unuseful and annoying, but hear me out and rock with me for a little bit. In these situations, we have left, been done, over it, and all of the adjectives that said this is finished before. In the beginning, it may have taken a lot to get to that point but as time has progressed, the amount of "over-it-ness" you can quickly possess may come pretty quickly. To the point that you've packed your bags, started making contingency plans, sought out ways of escape, and perhaps even physically moved. Yet in spite of all of that, you somehow find yourself right back in again. I can see you shaking your head and feeling some kind of way, I get it. I've done it. Don't beat yourself up. Here is the encouraging part, all of that is the beginning of the end. (That is also information I found out *AFTER* it'd ended!)

I'll use a bit of my story as an example. Prior to even getting married, I'd decided to end the whole relationship. In my mind, I'd already checked out and because I didn't want to deal with the law and courts and all that stuff, had decided that I would wait things out until the lease was up on the home I was renting and that would be the official departure of ways. I hadn't told anyone that was the plan, I was just going to carry it out. That was the beginning of the year in 2018, (remember

I got married in May). About a month after I'd made that decision a disastrous event took place and then came the grand epiphany. I bought what he was selling and we got married. During the marriage, when the straw finally broke the camel's back and we separated, I still kept a glimmer of hope, light, something to say, "Ok I know the separation will work and we'll have time to work out our differences, come to some real agreements and proceed forward." I was still wrong, but it goes back to what I said earlier, we just don't want to let go. After hearing that I could let go, it was a year later before I finally filed the papers to put the divorce in motion. During that time, I don't recall dangling the papers or taunting him with them. He would mention them to me and always left the conversation with hurt feelings when I would reply, "Well hurry up and file them so we can just be done."

By the time I'd actually taken the time to go to the court, file the papers, and have them served, I knew that I was at the point of no return. It was a "knowing" in my knower. I'd weighed the cost of continuing in our current manner to the price of being free and done with it. The first brought a feeling of dread; the second brought hope. I prayed it through and proceeded. The day I had the papers served was the day I took the ring off and on a 90-something-degree day in downtown Baltimore with no breeze in sight, I felt a cool one come across my face. When the divorce was finalized, I wanted to run around screaming but I couldn't, so I saved my celebration for church that Sunday and let loose.

It wasn't to celebrate the divorce. It was to celebrate the fact that I was and would remain free. It brings a whole new light to the verse, "Whom the Son sets free is free indeed," (John 8:36). These marriages are bondage, some weird form of modern-day demonic slavery. They are completely the opposite of Jeremiah 29:11.

Your Thoughts: Use this space for prayer, planning, and points of contact. Whether your instructions are to stay or to go, these are things you will need to aide you moving forward.

_____

_____

_____

_____

_____

_____

_____

_____

_____

_____

_____

_____

_____

_____

_____

_____

_____

_____

_____

_____

_____

_____

_____

_____

CHAPTER 9
Now What?

It is great to have information. It sounds nice. May even make you feel good. You come away empowered. But in the end, there's still that one nagging question, "Now what?!"

Well, friends, that's what teachers are for. To help you through those "Now what?" learning tasks. As I said at the beginning of the book, I am writing the book I needed. I don't buy into the "philosophy" that God put me in an abusive marriage. That's not His character. However, I strongly and firmly believe that He used what was sent to kill me for His glory. As a trained teacher, I look for the lessons in everything. This situation was no different. And because I find the lessons, I have to deliver them. So, in case I haven't told you, welcome to my classroom!

As a reminder, I am not a licensed therapist or counselor. I am a trained mental health coach who focuses on trauma-informed care and coaching. I implore you to please seek out licensed counsel to aid you. You've endured a lot. We all have. I am still realizing the magnitude of what I've gone through. Before I give you a list of steps or action items, we're going to pray. This journey will require you to be open, honest, and transparent, with God, yourself, and with others.

Dear Heavenly Father,

We come to you today to say Thank You. Thank You for being the amazing God that You are. Thank You for never leaving us. We thank You for sending help.

Lord, please open the heart and the mind of the reader of this book. Allow them to see, hear, and feel all that You will show them. Please help them to process what they have read and are reading. Just as You did for me, please send helpers to them that will cover them in prayer and walk with them through these trying times with no judgment.

Father God, I'm asking that You be the peace and comfort they need. Please meet every need they have and provide the resources they need to carry out Your will for their lives.

We give You all thanks, praise, honor, and glory.

In Jesus' Name,

Amen

Ok, you ready? Take a deep breath. Hold it for four, now let it out. Do it one more time. Whenever you begin to feel things are too much, go back to the deep breaths. Breathe in the goodness of God and the fact that He loves and cares about you. Breathe out any negative thoughts telling you that you can't or won't do any of this. You've got this!

The order is logical but not necessarily sequential, meaning it will make sense to do one thing before another but some of them can be done simultaneously. It's also important to remember that these are probably more tetrahedron-like rather than a circle or cycle. (Those 3-d type shapes that are all connected even though the pieces veer off to the sides, we'll make one for the resources!) These are not one-and-done completion items. They will be ongoing. The good news is that you will find that throughout the process you'll grow. For example, my Bible study life started by listening to the Bible every day on my way to work and back home. Now in my study time, I'm usually writing devotionals or full-out books to expand on what I'm reading and taking away from the verse(s). Give yourself the grace that you gave your spouse. You did not land here overnight; you will not come out overnight.

- **Create a personal bible study schedule.** – It's great to go to whatever mid-week service is offered by your church but this walk will require you to know what you

I Married Him NOW WHAT?

know on your own and for yourself. One of the ways the enemy works is to send people to you constantly quoting scripture inaccurately. However, if you haven't studied, you may not know that. I'll list some bible study ideas in the resources section.

- **Develop/rebuild your prayer life.** – I'm sure throughout this process you have prayed in some way, shape, or form. But now we're going to be more intentional about our prayers. One of the things I made it a point to begin doing, (and still do), was to change my prayers from asking for what I wanted to ask for God's will to be done. Honestly, accepting His will was tough in the beginning but the more I asked for it, the more I learned to be able to accept it and continue moving forward.

- **Consult the help of a professional.** – I started with a counselor. Over time, I also added a trauma-informed coach to my support system. The difference is that therapists, counselors, and doctors will have conversations with you that are strictly professional and solely rest on your journey of self-discovery. Coaches will do some of that as well, but coaches are allowed to share their personal experiences with you, not as advice but as examples. Licensed counselors will rarely speak to you about their personal lives or use themselves as examples. Some of you may be uncomfortable with the stigma attached to therapy. For so long we've been taught or told that seeing a professional negates our faith. It absolutely does not. There are saved, Holy Ghost-filled coaches and therapists who incorporate prayer, scripture, and discussions of faith into their practices.

- **Do not go into information overload.** – The amount of information regarding narcissistic abuse seems endless. Although in the beginning, it may seem refreshing to find information that you relate to, it can easily move from refreshing to overwhelming. When I first realized what I was dealing with I read everything I could, joined Facebook groups for support, followed blogs, and even researched in the actual DSM-5. While the research is comforting to a degree, it can also become disheartening. Read what you need to understand how to move and when you begin to feel it's too much, STOP!

- **Guard your gates.** – Pay close attention to what you watch, listen to, and who you decide to hold conversations with. I will not give you a list of "do-nots." We've heard those our whole lives. I'll give you an example. I used to post a lot of photos during my relationship on Facebook. While going through the divorce, those same photos began to make me feel angry because I realized the duality of them, (the smiling photo vs the horrid event that'd either taken place sometime before or shortly after the photo was taken). These fits of anger would keep me in a very weird and exhausting headspace from the time I saw the photo until hours later, and sometimes, into the next day. To stop dealing with these prolonged angry incidents, I just started deleting the photos.

- **Learn your triggers and react accordingly.** – One of the things our spouses love to do is push our buttons because they will take attention any way they can get it. Pay attention to things they pick at you about or constantly say to you to get a reaction. This is hard but you will have to learn not to react. Whenever my ex-husband wanted to get his way, he would never fail to mention how someone else did it or threaten to have someone else do it. I would yell, scream, and curse each time he did so. One day I just didn't respond, even though internally, I wanted to light him up! Everything with them is a power struggle. They have none and want to take yours. You control yourself and always have the power within. Your spouse can never take that from you. You just have to activate it.

- **Set and keep your boundaries.** – You do not have to set them all at once. In fact, you actually shouldn't. You won't be able to maintain them and once you cave on a boundary, it will become even more difficult to enforce the next one. But you have to start somewhere. My first boundary was enforcing how he would not speak to me. Each time he began cursing and screaming, he got one warning and then I'd end the convo. To this day, I still hold that boundary. There were others that took a little longer to enforce, however, over time, I still stand by them and have held them.

- **Find and use your circle of safety.** – It's no secret that this can easily become and may already be a very lonely experience, (especially if your spouse has succeeded in isolating you). When I felt there was no one I could talk to, I prayed for God to send someone who understood. While participating in a Facebook challenge, I met a group of women who have become my friends, sisters, and safe spaces. I also had the support of my family and my church family. In this space, be open to the fact that your circle may not initially be filled with people you know or have known.

These may be things that you've heard before and didn't feel like they would work or you're seeing them now for the first time and have the same feeling. I am writing as proof positive that it does. It's not easy but it's possible. We quote, "With God all things are possible," but then psych ourselves into believing that He's only possible to do everyone else's all things, not ours. That's a lie from the pit. These marriages may have been sent to keep us from our God-given destinies or to completely annihilate us mentally, emotionally, and in some cases physically. My prayer is that as you face your "Now What?" you do so knowing that you are not alone on this journey, help is available, and God is always near.

At this point, you may be realizing that divorce is imminent. I wanted to talk about grief and divorce in this book but it's way more involved, so it's looking like there will definitely be a book 4. What I will say for now, is to allow yourself to feel what you feel, process what you need to process, and grieve healthily.

Your Thoughts: *Take some time to think about your "Now what?"*

_____

_____

_____

_____

_____

_____

_____

_____

_____

_____

_____

_____

_____

_____

_____

_____

_____

_____

_____

_____

_____

CONCLUSION

In my closing ... There's not much more left to say. I am proud of you for reading through to the end. I am proud of you if you skipped around. I am proud of you if you started reading this page first! I'm proud of you period. Step one was picking up the book. Step two is application. With step three comes transformation.

You cannot change your spouse. You can pray for the renewing of their mind so that God can do the changing. You are allowed, encouraged, and empowered to be and become your best you. You don't need your spouse's permission. You don't need my permission. God already gave you freedom. You just have to walk in it.

Whether you choose to stay or leave, I pray the information presented here helps you make the best choice for you. Don't forget to check out the resources section.

Your homework ... Work through the steps. If you need help, or coach class as I used to offer my students, my info is on the resources page. See you next class!

Your Thoughts: *Lasting impressions. You made it to the end, what are you thinking, feeling, all the things?*

_____

_____

_____

_____

_____

_____

_____

_____

_____

_____

_____

_____

_____

_____

_____

_____

_____

_____

_____

_____

_____

_____

_____

_____

RESOURCES

Follow the QR code below to be taken to the Resources Page. It's full of information, other books that helped me, as well as information on counselors and coaches. Also, some other links such as how to make a Tetrahedron and one of my praise and worship playlists.

ABOUT THE AUTHOR

Takhia Gaither decided during the pandemic that there would be no more hiding! To date she has co-authored over 10 anthologies, 3 of which were Amazon Bestsellers in multiple categories, written and created a Bible Study Workbook – *Be the Overcomer*, written for various online publications, created lined inspirational journals, both yearly and financial planners, and currently maintains two blogs. In the fall of 2022, she launched the Redefining Thoughts Podcast and YouTube shows. Her portfolio continues to grow with new book projects to be unveiled beginning in the spring of 2023, in addition to becoming an international TEDx speaker and curriculum writer and moving into traveling as a speaker, teacher, and coach.

Takhia is a mother, retired educator, author, editor, and certified Christian Confidence and Mental Health Coach, with a specialization in trauma-informed coaching to be completed summer of 2023. Writing has always been a hobby, so in 2018 she began her blog, *Takhia the Teacher,* and began writing as a volunteer for the online publication *Godly Today.* She started The Ready Write-Her editing, copywriting, and formatting company in 2019 as a profitable hobby. With the release of her first anthology, *She Changed Her Narrative,* she also became a published editor. Throughout the process of writing, she received countless confirmations that her years of teaching were moving her from public school to the classroom of life. In addition to editing, she is also a writing coach for new authors who seek training and accountability as they prepare their stories for the world to see. Follow her on the web and on social media:

Web – thereadywrite-her.com

Blogs – tsgsgroup.com/redefiningyou
        takhiatheteacher.wixsite.com/ttheteach

Facebook, Instagram & Pinterest – takhiatheteacher

YouTube – bit.ly/redefiningthoughts
         bit.ly/TakhiaTheTeacher

E-Mail – thereadywrite-her@tsgsgroup.com

Need to talk?? Bit.ly/TakhiasCalendar

www.ingramcontent.com/pod-product-compliance
Lightning Source LLC
Chambersburg PA
CBHW060331130626
46553CB00003B/967